Christmas Traditions

Christmas Traditions

Making Your Family Celebrations Memorable

Stan and Linda Toler
Elmer and Ruth Towns

Beacon Hill Press of Kansas City
Kansas City, Missouri

Copyright 1998
by Beacon Hill Press of Kansas City

ISBN 083-411-7169

Printed in the
United States of America

Cover Design: Paul Franitza
Cover Photo: Comstock

Library of Congress Cataloging-in-Publication Data
Christmas traditions : making your family celebrations memo-
    rable / Stan Toler . . . [et al.].
        p.   cm.
    ISBN 0-8341-1716-9 (pbk.)
    1. Christmas—United States.   2. United States—Social
life and customs.   I. Toler, Stan.
GT4986.A1C475   1998
394.2663'0973—dc21   98-24638
                                                              CIP

10   9   8   7   6   5   4   3   2   1

SPECIAL THANKS
Mechelle Fain, Mark Hollingsworth, Derl Keefer,
Kelly Gallagher, Bruce Nuffer, and Michael Estep

Introduction

Christmas traditions prepare our hearts to celebrate the birth of Jesus. Without traditions, each year would be an uncharted path. We wouldn't know what to expect.

Christmas traditions give anticipation to every December. We decorate evergreen trees, purchase presents, and travel home. Christmas carols, Nativity scenes, and Handel's *Messiah* all stir our souls. Christmas sits on our shoulder and flirts with us, tempting us to embrace the season.

Christmas traditions are hot apple cider, cranberry sauce, wise men, Grandma's house, and vacation from work . . . jingle bells and "dashing through the snow." Everyone enjoys such traditions, and so do we. Yours are just as wonderful as ours because they stir your spirit, just as we get "warm fuzzies" dreaming about ours. We've opened our hearts to you, so you can look into our pasts and be inspired to treasure Christmas all the more.

May our Christmas traditions help your traditions become more meaningful. May everything we remember about Christmas make us say with the wise men, "Where is the one who has been born king of the Jews? We saw his star in the east and have come to worship him" (Matt. 2:2).

Remembering,
Stan and Linda from Oklahoma City
Elmer and Ruth from Lynchburg, Virginia

7

Hath not old custom
made this life more sweet?

—Shakespeare

Christmas
Reflections

A Family Litany

Leader: And there were shepherds living out in the fields nearby, keeping watch over their flocks at night.

Family: An angel of the Lord appeared to them, and the glory of the Lord shone around them, and they were terrified.

Leader: But the angel said to them, "Do not be afraid. I bring you good news of great joy that will be for all the people.

Family: "Today in the town of David a Savior has been born to you; he is Christ the Lord.

Leader: "This will be a sign to you: You will find a baby wrapped in cloths and lying in a manger."

Family: Suddenly a great company of the heavenly host appeared with the angel, praising God and saying,

Leader: "Glory to God in the highest, and on earth peace to men on whom his favor rests."

Family: When the angels had left them and gone into heaven, the shepherds said to one another, "Let's go to

11

Bethlehem and see this thing that has happened, which the Lord has told us about."

Leader: So they hurried off and found Mary and Joseph, and the baby, who was lying in the manger.

Family: When they had seen him, they spread the word concerning what had been told them about this child,

Leader: and all who heard it were amazed at what the shepherds said to them. But Mary treasured up all these things and pondered them in her heart.

Family: The shepherds returned, glorifying and praising God for all the things they had heard and seen, which were just as they had been told.

—Luke 2:8-20

Secrets and Surprises

Somehow, not only for Christmas
But all the long year through,
The joy that you give to others
Is the joy that comes back to you.

—John Greenleaf Whittier

*I*t is more blessed to give than to receive." Our family
has learned this important lesson. Each member of our
extended family goes to his or her overflowing closets,
toy boxes, or pantries to find presents for a family who
might not have Christmas. After deciding who will receive the surprise gifts, we sneak information such as
sizes, ages of children, or specific needs. Next, we collect
a large box of goodies—lotions or fragrances for Mom,
warm sweaters and a toy for each child, something special for Dad, and a bag or two of groceries—a ham, oranges and nuts, a package of dressing, some sweet pota-
toes, freshly baked bread, and a few candies to top it off.

Christmas Eve night, we decide who will have the
honor of delivering the gifts. Amid giggles, barking

dogs, and tripping over each other, the delivery team leaves the box on the doorstep, rings the bell, and runs like crazy. This is always so much fun, we now fight over who gets to deliver the surprise.

One year we received a big cardboard thank-you card in our gift-family's front yard. It said, "Thank you, Santa, whoever you are."

—Elmer and Ruth Towns

It is in giving that we receive.

—Francis of Assisi

After Annunciation

This is the irrational season
When love blooms bright and wild.
Had Mary been filled with reason
There'd have been no room for the child.

—Madeleine L'Engle

Little Plastic Jesus

*H*e's been in the attic for 11 long months. Stuffed in an old shoe box with cows, sheep, angels, wise men, shepherds, and his folks. Now his time has come. For the little plastic Jesus, it's out of the attic and onto the mantel.

For a month he'll be prominently displayed, but then it will all be over. Once again he will be wrapped in tissue, stuffed back into the shoe box, and carted off to the attic. The routine is so familiar, and in the midst of the routine, the wonder surrounding the real Jesus can be elusive. Could it be true that the little plastic Jesus is the better recognized of the two?

The little plastic Jesus is lovable but lifeless. The last prophet, John the Baptist, announced, "Among you stands one you do not know" (John 1:26). The little plastic Jesus, shoe box resident, attic prisoner, can never be known. No life is possible in and through him.

But the real Jesus, who conquered death's prison, is seated forever at the Father's right hand. He can be known. Paul said, "I want to know Christ" (Phil. 3:10). John said, "In him was life, and that life was the light of men" (John 1:4).

—Terry Toler
(Stan's brother)

Reflections from a 13-Year-Old

For to us a child is born,
to us a son is given,
and the government will be on his shoulders.
And he will be called
Wonderful Counselor, Mighty God,
Everlasting Father, Prince of Peace.

—Isa. 9:6

In our gloom and despair, we often fear that our sorrows and troubles are endless. But we can take comfort in knowing that even though the Lord doesn't always take us around our troubles, He will lead us safely through them if we follow Him with all our heart.

Isa. 9:2 says, "The people walking in darkness have seen a great light; on those living in the land of the shadow of death a light has dawned." Jesus was and forever will be the Light of the World. When Jesus came down from heaven, His holy love shone through the darkness until the darkness was no more.

—Seth Toler
Nashville (1991)

Reflections from Children

Trinity Church of the Nazarene, 1997
Pastor Stan Toler

Welcome everyone!
I came up here to tell you this,
My Christmas gift is one sweet kiss!

—written by Loretta Hollingsworth (Stan's mother). Presented by
Stan Toler (age 4), The Tabernacle, Baileysville, West Virginia.

My favorite thing about Christmas is when I give
to others. I also like it when Mommy and Daddy hide
baby Jesus from the Nativity scene and we go find him
Christmas morning.

—Caylee Retter, age 8

At Christmastime I like to get lots of presents, but
the best thing about Christmas is Jesus.

—Austin Griffin, age 7

I love Christmas presents, and I love Jesus.

—Jana Johnson, age 8

My favorite thing to do at Christmas is to open the presents. But the best thing about Christmas is the birth of Christ Jesus.

—Jenae Johnson, age 9

Jesus Loves Me

Jesus loves me! this I know,
For the Bible tells me so.
Little ones to Him belong;
They are weak, but He is strong.

—Anna B. Warner

Christmas Day, 1981, Heritage Memorial Church.

She carried her beginner's book and slowly approached the grand piano, left center of the platform. Kim Hawk was all of 10 years old—a Down syndrome child.

More than a thousand worshipers silently cheered for her as she opened the book and began to play the

Sunday morning offertory. With one finger, Kim painstakingly pecked out "Jesus Loves Me." At times she paused indefinitely, struggling to place her stubby little fingers on the right keys. Her brow wrinkled in concentration, her lips puckered with determination, her eyes narrowed with intensity.

As Kim continued in her simple, pure worship, my own heart swelled with God's love—perfect, holy, blameless. "Yes, Jesus loves me. / Yes, Jesus loves me. / Yes, Jesus loves me. / The Bible tells me so." Every nuance of Christmas seemed wrapped in that simple message.

At last, Kim finished and slipped off the piano bench. An avalanche of applause punctuated her message. "Jesus loves me!" swelled from every heart as God's Spirit filled that sanctuary with the force of His infinite power. Grown men, breathing deeply, struggled to retain their dignity while weepy women searched for tissues to blot their damp cheeks.

As He invaded the world 2,000 years before, the holy Creator invaded our church service through the simplicity of an innocent child. God was near. And in that close moment, He wrapped His arms around each of us and simply said, "I love you."

—Stan Toler

We'll Bring Our Hearts

The wise may bring their learning;
The rich may bring their wealth.
And some may bring their greatness;
And some bring strength and health.
We, too, would bring our treasures
To offer to the King:
We have no wealth or learning;
What shall we children bring?

We'll bring Him hearts that love Him;
We'll bring Him thankful praise
And young souls meekly striving
To walk in holy ways:
And these shall be the treasures
We offer to the King;
And these are gifts that even
The poorest child may bring.

—Anonymous

My Favorite Christmas Memory

by third graders at Bethany Elementary School
Linda Toler, teacher

*M*y favorite Christmas memory is when we open the presents and when I am with my family. I like my presents. I feel very happy all day. I give thanks to God that none of my family is dead and my teacher. I like playing in the snow with my cousins, sisters, and brothers. And sitting by the fireplace. I have enjoyed Christmas all these years. I get to know how they really are. I want to have a very good Christmas this year.

Love, Anna Hernandez

*M*y favorite Christmas was when Austin and Lisa came over. We got lots of great gifts. We went rollerblading around the block. Then we went to the park and asked the police if we could build a snowman. After we built one, we went home and drank some hot cocoa with our lunch. For a snack we ate fresh homemade cookies. Then we watched some movies. After the movies we wrote Christmas cards and packed candy sacks for poor kids and orphans. It breaks my heart to see sad faces. That's the end.

—Jamie Drury

My favorite Christmas memory is when I get to spend time with my family. We decorate the tree, go shopping, and go caroling. After we have our Christmas cookies, we go to the Christmas Eve service at church. I usually sit on the third pew. I love to watch my mom play the organ. The choir sings beautiful songs, and the congregation lights white candles. After the Christmas Eve service, we go to bed. The next morning we open our presents. We're all in for a big surprise!

—Abby Broyles

The Legend of the Christmas Rose

Legend says that a little shepherd girl of Bethlehem followed after the shepherds who had received the angels' message and were journeying to the stable. All the shepherds took along gifts for the Christ child; but the little girl had no gift to give. As she lagged behind the others, somewhat sad at heart, there suddenly appeared an angel in a glow of light, who scattered beautiful white roses in her path. Eagerly she gathered them in her arms and laid them at the manger as her gift to the little Lord Jesus.

23

We all have love and joy to give.
And what a joy life is to live
If we just scatter everywhere
The things God's given us to share.
If you have a gift—bring it.
If you have a song—sing it.
If you have a talent—use it.
If you have love—diffuse it.
If you have gladness—share it.
If you have happiness—give it.
If you have religion—live it.
If you have a prayer—pray it.

—Author unknown

Christ has
No body now on earth but yours;
No hands but yours;
No feet but yours;
Yours are the eyes
Through which is to look out
Christ's compassion to the world;
Yours are the feet
With which He is to go about
Doing good.

Paul M. Bassett, *Keep the Wonder* (Kansas City: Beacon Hill Press of Kansas City, 1979), 24.

The Truth About Santa

Saint Nicholas was born wealthy in A.D. 280. He was a small-town boy from Patara in Asia Minor. Even though an epidemic killed his parents during his youth, they had made sure of both his spiritual and material wealth. Nicholas had a faith no one could shake.

After his parents' death, Nicholas lived in Myra and there showed his love for Christ through his love for others. Eventually, the town asked him to be its bishop. Emperor Diocletian jailed him because of his faith. But Emperor Constantine released him.

News of Saint Nicholas's generous deeds spread through the countryside. Not only did he beg for food for the poor, but he also gave impoverished girls dowries which enabled them to find husbands. And, of course, there is the unforgettable story of his putting on a costume, sneaking into the homes of poor children, and leaving gifts. Because of his generosity, Nicholas gave away everything he owned and died poor in 314.

He never rode around with reindeer, though. We can thank the clergyman Clement Clarke Moore for that (1822). And if you like his suit, you can thank the illustrator Thomas Nast for that. But for his generosity and love, you can thank his Heavenly Father.

Saint Nicholas is the embodiment of what we all

should be. The man reached out to his world and has touched humanity ever since. Think what our world would be like if we followed his example.

Maybe this is the Santa that parents should tell their children about. Perhaps telling youngsters the real story of Santa would put the right balance into the Christmas gift-giving ritual.

Debra White Smith, *The Dallas Morning News*, Friday, November 24, 1994. Used by permission.

A Front Door Santa

When the children were little, construction paper pieces made a wonderful Santa for the front door. Each year we all helped put Santa together. First we covered the door with solid red wrapping paper. Then we added paper, fur, eyes, a beard, and buttons. The belt and boots we cut from black paper. The children and I thought our door Santa was a work of art, and we enjoyed him for many years. Part of his appeal was his noticeable child-made charm. Neighborhood children also enjoyed him, and we soon saw paper Santas on other doors.

As our children got older, the decorations became nicer, more dignified, and more expensive. But the one we remember most was the one we made together from scraps of construction paper.

—Ruth Towns

A mother discovered her five-year-old daughter drawing with her crayons on some paper. "What are you drawing?" she asked.

"A picture of God," the little girl said.

The mother replied, "No one knows what God looks like."

"They will when I get through."

'Twas the Night Before Christmas

'Twas the night before Christmas,
when all through the house
Not a creature was stirring,
—not even a mouse;
The stockings were hung by the chimney with care,
In hopes that St. Nicholas soon would be there.
The children were nestled all snug in their beds
While visions of sugarplums danced in their heads;
And Mama in her kerchief and I in my cap,
Had just settled down for a long winter's nap—

When out on the lawn there rose such a clatter,
I sprang from my bed to see what was the matter.
Away to the window I flew like a flash,
Tore open the shutters and threw up the sash.
The moon on the breast of the new-fallen snow,
Gave a luster of midday to objects below;
When, what to my wondering eyes should appear,
But a miniature sleigh and eight tiny reindeer,
With a little old driver so lively and quick,
I knew in a moment it must be St. Nick.

More rapid than eagles his coursers they came,
And he whistled, and shouted,
and called them by name—
"Now, Dasher! Now, Dancer!
Now, Prancer and Vixen!
On, Comet! On, Cupid! On, Donder and Blitzen!
To the top of the porch, to the top of the wall!
Now, dash away! Dash away! Dash away all!"
As the dry leaves before the wild hurricane fly,
When they meet with an obstacle, mount to the sky,
So up to the housetop the coursers they flew,
With sleigh full of toys—and St. Nicholas too;
And then in a twinkling, I heard on the roof
The prancing and pawing of each little hoof.

As I drew in my head and was turning around,
Down the chimney St. Nicholas came with a bound.
He was dressed all in fur from his head to his foot,
And his clothes were all tarnished
with ashes and soot.
A bundle of toys he had flung on his back,
And he looked like a peddler just opening his pack.
His eyes how they twinkled! His dimples how merry!
His cheeks were like roses, his nose like a cherry.
His droll little mouth was drawn up like a bow,
And the beard on his chin was as white as the snow!
The stump of a pipe he held tight in his teeth,
And the smoke it encircled his head like a wreath.
He had a broad face and a little round belly
That shook when he laughed like a bowl full of jelly.
He was chubby and plump—a right jolly old elf,
And I laughed when I saw him, in spite of myself.

A wink of his eye and a twist of his head,
Soon gave me to know I had nothing to dread.
He spoke not a word, but went straight to his work,
And filled all the stockings then turned with a jerk,
And laying his finger aside of his nose,
And giving a nod, up the chimney he rose.

He sprang to his sleigh, to his team gave a whistle,
And away they all flew like the down of a thistle.
But I heard him exclaim as he drove out of sight,
"Happy Christmas to all, and to all a good-night!"
Clement Clarke Moore, "A Visit from St. Nicholas" (Troy, New York), 1822.

Cookies and Milk

It's good to be children sometimes, and never better than at Christmas when its Mighty Founder was a child Himself.

—Charles Dickens

$\mathcal{D}$ecember can be hectic with the lists, hurried shoppers, baking, parties, and all the gift wrapping. In our house, we treasure the evenings after the children are tucked in bed, and the adults can relax in front of the fire with a cup of flavored coffee or cappuccino.

Believing Santa's life is a little rushed and hectic, too, we always help the children provide cookies and milk for our Christmas Eve visitor. One year, our granddaughter Tammy even created a special Christmas plate for Santa's food. Leaving a midnight snack for St. Nicholas excites the children.

On Christmas morning they loved to wake up to discover crumbs or an almost empty milk glass to prove the old gentleman enjoyed their snack. However, Santa recently left a note that said due to the chilly night, he would prefer hot chocolate, or especially coffee, not cold milk. The last few years, Santa has not left even one drop of his warm drink.

P.S. Cream, no sugar.

—Elmer Towns

Stocking Stuffers

God's gifts put man's best dreams to shame.

—Elizabeth Barrett Browning

Traditionally, Elmer shops for the stocking stuffers. Every family member and visitor must put out a stocking to be filled by "Santa" on Christmas Eve. Elmer will fill 17 stockings this year! Next year, there'll be 18! Elmer loves filling the stockings. He gives toothbrushes, shoe polish, a comb, and always the book of LifeSavers. He waits until Christmas Eve to shop but always has more than enough gifts. One of the men is sure to receive the traditional balsa airplane.

Everyone's stocking is different. When grandchildren are born, it's fun to see what kind of sock they will receive. Our granddaughter, baby Collyn, has white satin, just the right size. Ruth's stocking is deep wine velvet. Grandpa Forbes always used his big, old work socks. Grandma claimed her panty hose didn't really hold more gifts, but she was pleased when "Santa" filled both legs. Everyone's name is permanently attached to his or her Christmas sock, and each year we unpack them for another Christmas Eve filling.

The rule is, you may open your stocking first, but the other gifts wait until everyone is present.

—Elmer and Ruth Towns

I, Too, Must Sing

Ah, dearest Jesus, holy Child,
Make Thee a bed, soft, undefiled,
Within my heart that it may be
A quiet chamber kept for Thee.
My heart for very joy doth leap,
My lips no more can silence keep,

I, too, must sing with joyful tongue
That sweetest ancient cradle song:
"Glory to God in the highest heaven,
Who unto man His Son hath given."
While angels sing with pious mirth
A glad new year to all the earth.

—Martin Luther

Presents endear absents.

—Charles Lamb

What Child Is This?

What Child is this who, laid to rest,
On Mary's lap is sleeping?
Whom angels greet with anthems sweet,
While shepherds watch are keeping?

This, this is Christ, the King,
Whom shepherds guard and angels sing.
Haste, haste to bring Him laud,
The Babe, the Son of Mary.

—William C. Dix (1865)

34

Hark! the Herald Angels Sing

Hark! the herald angels sing,
"Glory to the newborn King!
Peace on earth, and mercy mild—
God and sinners reconciled."
Joyful, all ye nations, rise;
Join the triumph of the skies.
With th' angelic host proclaim,
"Christ is born in Bethlehem."
Hark! the herald angels sing,
"Glory to the newborn King."

—Charles Wesley (1739)

Music

*C*hills run up and down my spine at the opening notes of the "Hallelujah" chorus. "Chestnuts Roasting on an Open Fire" gives me warm "hot chocolate" feelings. "Jingle Bells" and "Deck the Halls" leave me jolly, but I'm drawn to worship with "O Little Town of Bethlehem" or "What Child Is This?"

Each year we add to our Christmas music collection and start the CDs early in the day for hours of background music. We enjoy everything from Neil Diamond to Doug Oldham, and the *Nutcracker* to *A Country Christmas*.

—Ruth Towns

God's Night-Light

The angels sang a song of peace
That night so long ago
To tell us God had sent goodwill,
To set the world aglow.

The first to hear that blessed song
Were shepherds on a hill.
While in the dark they watched their sheep,
That song their hearts did thrill.

They went to see the One God sent
To bring to all men light.
There in a manger lay the Babe
Who came to banish night.

The wise men lived long miles away,
But God gave them a star;
And in the night they traveled on
Through dark the road and far.

And so God has a star or song
To guide us on His way,
Glad in our night we follow on
To God's Eternal Day.

Leah Whitnall Smith, "God's Night Light," *Advent Devotional* (A devotional book published by Nashville First Church of the Nazarene, November, 1985), 23. Used by permission.

Jesus Christ was born *into* this world, not *from* it. He did not emerge out of history; He came into history from the outside.

—Oswald Chambers

The Light of the World Is Jesus

Come to the Light; 'tis shining for thee.
Sweetly the Light has dawned upon me.
Once I was blind, but now I can see.
The Light of the world is Jesus.

—Philip P. Bliss (1875)

In the beginning was the Word, and the Word was with God, and the Word was God. He was with God in the beginning. Through him all things were made; without him nothing was made that has been made. In him was life, and that life was the light of men. The light shines in the darkness, but the darkness has not understood it.

—*John 1:1-5*

Christmas Bunny

Were earth a thousand times as fair,
Beset with gold and jewels rare,
She yet were far too poor to be
A narrow cradle, Lord, for Thee.

—Martin Luther

*M*y friend Bunny Marks and I didn't have much money, but we wanted to make things beautiful. Therefore, we discovered gold spray paint as a definite Christmas necessity. Together, we picked weeds and pods, pinecones and branches. After spraying them gold, we arranged them just so. Each arrangement looked as though a florist had worked magic.

One year we cut a bare tree branch, touched it up with white shoe polish, sprayed it with hair spray, and sprinkled it with sugar. We hung the "frosted" branch over the fireplace, and the room was transformed into a winter wonderland. The next Christmas, Bunny and I frosted another tree branch and added a little gold bird.

We could hardly wait to use our creativity from one Christmas to the next. Bunny lives in heaven now, but sometimes when I use gold spray paint or powdered sugar, I thank the Lord for her. She never thought my ideas were dumb. Bunny saw beauty in simple things. We all saw beauty in Bunny.

—Ruth Towns

Joy to the World

Joy to the world! the Lord is come;
Let earth receive her King.
Let ev'ry heart prepare Him room,

And heav'n and nature sing,
And heav'n and nature sing,
And heav'n, and heav'n and nature sing.

—Isaac Watts (1719)

Doesn't Everybody?

Doesn't everybody start their decorating the first day of December? We do, then add something each day until Christmas—a new ornament, a candle, another angel, another bell, or a stocking for the newest baby. The best part of decorating is finding the oldest ornament, the star for the treetop. The star is tarnished now, but a dash of gold spray paint makes it look as good as new.

I love the first day of December! It signals the beginning of our joyous festivities. All the stores start decorating earlier every year, but we wait until December 1. It's *tradition!*

—Ruth Towns

How "Silent Night" Was Born

"Silent Night" was written on Christmas Eve, 1818, in Oberndorf, Austria, near Salzburg. A hungry mouse had eaten through the leather of the organ bellows, so Joseph Mohr, the priest, and Franz Gruber, the organist, had to compose a carol for children's voices and guitar on short notice. The fame of "Silent Night" spread slowly and by a series of coincidences throughout the world, but it was not until 1867 that the song was published under the names of its true composers. By then, both men were dead.

At Christmas the love of God and the love of our family overcomes the hatred, pain, and greed in our world. The peace of Jesus Christ brings comfort instead of stress.

—Linda Toler

Cheerful Mailbox

*I*f I were a mail carrier, I would prefer a decorated mailbox. The cheerful greeting would make mail delivery more enjoyable. There's something pleasurable about encountering a mailbox decorated for the holidays. We decorate from our mailbox near the street, all the way to the house. Martha Stewart suggests that we share Christmas joy by making our yards festive and inviting. This includes the mailbox. Ours gets greenery and a big gold bow. The shiny bow reflects light at night and glistens in the sunlight all day. Our grandchildren have added their own decorations in recent years—a toy tied into the ribbon, or bells that tinkle when the wind blows.

—Ruth Towns

Then Isaiah said, "Hear now, you house of David! Is it not enough to try the patience of men? Will you try the patience of my God also? Therefore the Lord himself will give you a sign: The virgin will be with child and will give birth to a son, and will call him Immanuel."

—Isa. 7:13-14

In that day there will be an altar to the LORD in the heart of Egypt, and a monument to the LORD at its border. It will be a sign and witness to the LORD Almighty in the land of Egypt. When they cry out to the Lord because of their oppressors, he will send them a savior and defender, and he will rescue them. So the LORD will make himself known to the Egyptians, and in that day they will acknowledge the LORD.

—Isa. 19:19-21

Here is my servant, whom I uphold,
my chosen one in whom I delight;
I will put my Spirit on him
and he will bring justice to the nations.
He will not shout or cry out,
or raise his voice in the streets.
A bruised reed he will not break,
and a smoldering wick he will not snuff out.
In faithfulness he will bring forth justice;
he will not falter or be discouraged
till he establishes justice on earth.
In his law the islands will put their hope.

—Isa. 42:1-4

How beautiful on the mountains
are the feet of those who bring good news,
who proclaim peace,
who bring good tidings,
who proclaim salvation,
who say to Zion,
"Your God reigns!"

—*Isa. 52:7*

Sneaky Snooper

Thanks be to God for his indescribable gift!

—*2 Cor. 9:15*

I'm a snooper—always have been, always will be.
Elmer wraps a gift on December 1 and tantalizes me for
25 days. So I am adept at unwrapping and rewrapping
without any telltale evidence.

My Christmas snooping started when I was six
years old, and I discovered Santa's hiding place. I saw

roller skates that were too small for my big brother. For weeks, I secretively giggled with the knowledge. My find brought me such sweet satisfaction. I've snooped every year since. After 60 years, I'm a champion snooper!

But even though I'm a champion snooper, I don't allow anybody else to be! I hide my gifts in the most absurd spots and then place them in exact position so I can tell if they've been disturbed. I may align the edge of a package with the edge of the shelf or set a pin on top of it. So I'm really more of a sneaky snooper!

—Ruth Towns

The Work of Christmas

When the song of the angels is stilled,
When the star in the sky is gone,
When the kings and princes are home,
When the shepherds are back with their flock,
The work of Christmas begins:
To find the lost,
To heal the broken,
To feed the hungry,

To release the prisoner,
To rebuild the nations,
To bring peace among brothers,
To make music in the heart.

—Author unknown

*Y*ou who bring good tidings to Zion, go up on a high mountain. You who bring good tidings to Jerusalem, lift up your voice with a shout, lift it up, do not be afraid; say to the towns of Judah,

"Here is your God!"

See, the Sovereign LORD comes with power, and his arm rules for him. See, his reward is with him, and his recompense accompanies him. He tends his flock like a shepherd: He gathers the lambs in his arms and carries them close to his heart; he gently leads those that have young.

—Isa. 40:9-11

Go, Tell It on the Mountain

Go, tell it on the mountain,
Over the hills and ev'rywhere;
Go, tell it on the mountain
That Jesus Christ is born!

While shepherds kept their watching
O'er silent flocks by night,
Behold! Thro'out the heavens
There shone a holy light.

Go, tell it on the mountain,
Over the hills and ev'rywhere;
Go, tell it on the mountain
That Jesus Christ is born!

—John W. Work Jr.

The Inflated Intruder

Guide me in your truth and teach me, for you are God my Savior, and my hope is in you all day long.

—Ps. 25:5

*L*ong ago we lived in an airy old house that creaked and moaned like an old person. We got used to the noises, but one Christmas Eve our family thought we had an intruder, and it wasn't Santa!

Elmer carefully placed all the gifts around the tree before coming to bed. Some toys were left unwrapped so little eyes would open wide with excitement upon first glimpses of the living room.

The family was asleep. The dark house was quiet except for the usual cracking and creaking.

Suddenly, something fell, a bell jingled, and a baby doll cried. We sprang from our beds to see what was the matter. Elmer was in the lead. "OK, who's there?" he demanded. Baseball bat in hand, he entered the living room and turned on the light to discover the inflated pink and green reindeer had deflated, collapsed, and knocked over several toys.

The kids were huddled behind their bedroom doors, so they didn't even get a sneak preview of the Christmas gifts. All they wanted to know was that their Dad was in control. The pink and green inflatable intruder was as flat as a pancake and no more a threat to our safety.

—Ruth Towns

Gabriel's Surprise Announcement to Zechariah

He will be a joy and delight to you, and many will rejoice because of his birth, for he will be great in the sight of the Lord. He is never to take wine or other fermented drink, and he will be filled with the Holy Spirit even from birth. Many of the people of Israel will he bring back to the Lord their God. And he will go on before the Lord, in the spirit and power of Elijah, to turn the hearts of the fathers to their children and the disobedient to the wisdom of the righteous—to make ready a people prepared for the Lord.

—Luke 1:14-17

Come, Thou long-expected Jesus,
Born to set Thy people free.
From our fears and sins release us;
Let us find our rest in Thee.
Israel's Strength and Consolation,
Hope of all the earth Thou art—
Dear Desire of ev'ry nation,
Joy of ev'ry longing heart!

Born Thy people to deliver,
Born a Child and yet a King,
Born to reign in us forever,
Now Thy gracious kingdom bring.
By Thine own eternal Spirit,
Rule in all our hearts alone.
By Thine all-sufficient merit,
Raise us to Thy glorious throne.

—Charles Wesley

A "Beary" Merry Christmas

When Elmer goes on trips, he brings home bears. I have sleep shirts with bears on them and a clock with bears on the face. I also have about 12 dozen stuffed bears of all shapes, sizes, and colors. The grandchildren love to help me at Christmastime because the bears get Santa hats, bows on top of their heads, or ribbons around their necks. A few stuffed bears may hold an ornament or bell, but all are properly decked out in holiday finery. This year the bears have their own little Christmas tree with an angel bear at the top and ornament bears as decoration.

My biggest bear, the size of a six-year-old child, came 15 years ago. Elmer and I saw him while out Christmas shopping, but he was too expensive. When Elmer went back on Christmas Eve, the bear was still waiting for us, so Elmer bargained and got it for half price. He put the bear in the child's seat of the shopping basket and headed for the checkout.

A fellow shopper jokingly asked the name of his child.

"Teddy," Elmer shot back, and Teddy is still his name.

—Ruth Towns

Puzzling Rugs

*W*e have the most unique padding you could imagine under our rugs. Some people sweep dirt under rugs or hide other secrets there, but we have puzzles under every rug in the house. You see, each December a puzzle "appears" on the coffee table. Family and friends all help put it together. After completing the puzzle, we turn it over, sign it, date it, and tape it together. Under the rug it goes, along with puzzles of snow babies, Santa drinking Coke, a Monet, and 17 others under the dining room, living-room, entry, and family room rugs. (Our guests have also discovered a "puzzle in progress" under the tablecloth in the dining room.)

—Elmer and Ruth Towns

Your attitude should be the same
as that of Christ Jesus:
Who, being in very nature God,
did not consider equality with God something
to be grasped,
but made himself nothing,
taking the very nature of a servant,
being made in human likeness.

And being found in appearance as a man,
he humbled himself
and became obedient to death—
even death on a cross!

—Phil. 2:5-8

Giving Without Receiving

Since 1984, Seth, Adam, and I have enjoyed visiting our church's shut-ins on Christmas Eve day. Linda carefully helps us plan gifts for each of our friends. Usually we take homemade peanut brittle, a red poinsettia, and a book.

Once in the car, I always explain to the boys that they will be giving and not receiving gifts at the homes we visit. (Of course, we usually accept some cider and cookies if offered!)

When we are ready to leave, we sing a Christmas carol and pray with our friends. Invariably we feel blessed for the moments that we spend with each person.

—Stan Toler

Give, and it will be given to you.
A good measure,
pressed down, shaken together
and running over,
will be poured into your lap.
For with the measure you use,
it will be measured to you.

—*Luke 6:38*

A Package a Day Keeps Gloom Away

*O*ur grandchildren, Beth and Kim, love to visit their Grandma and Grandpa Wooldridge. From December 1 to Christmas, the girls receive a gift from a special stocking every day they visit.

—Ruth Towns

A little nonsense now and then
Is relished by the wisest men!

—Mary Michael

One at a Time

Elmer wants gift exchanging to last. After all, we shop for months, decorate for weeks, wrap gifts for days, cook for hours, and gift opening is over in minutes. Not so with Elmer in charge. On Christmas morning he gives each person a gift to hold; then we open one gift at a time, beginning with the youngest.

"Who is it from?" Elmer asks. "Can you guess what it is?"

Then Elmer gives permission to open. After "Ooooooh" and "Aaaaaah" and "Thank you," he goes to the next oldest person.

"Who is it from? . . . Can you guess what it is? . . . OK, you may open."

We wiggle and squirm because opening gifts Elmer-style takes forever. Everyone shares in the excitement that lasts about two hours. But who's in a hurry? Christmas only comes once a year.

—Ruth Towns

For God so loved the world that he
gave his one and only Son,
that whoever believes in him shall not perish
but have eternal life.

—John 3:16

58

Let the Begging Begin

We knew it would happen. We knew what the answer would be. But best of all was to watch the way the begging began.

The kids made sure Dad was comfortable in his favorite chair. They lighted the candles and played Christmas music. I brought him a huge bowl of popcorn and a frosty mug of root beer. He would smile. He knew he was being set up.

Soon Debbie would say, "Hey, Dad, I know something you don't know. I know what's in your package."

Polly and Sam would join in, "I know what you're getting. Don't you wish you knew?"

Then Sam would begin the "butter-up." "Dad, you know, I've been thinking what a great dad you've been this year. Thanks, Dad."

Before Sam was finished, little Polly would crawl into Dad's lap and begin her cuddles and kisses. Soon she would begin, "Daddy, could we please open just one present tonight?" "Please, please, please, pu-leee-zzz!"

With all that schmoozing, only Scrooge himself would say no.

—Ruth Towns

A Gift of Memories

Joy comes to you at Christmas
by inviting Jesus into your heart.

—Jeffrey Johnson

Do you remember what you got or gave for Christmas last year? These last few years, we decided to give some lasting memories to our family. We save our money all year and take the whole family on a trip.

Each person receives a disposable camera, even the little ones. We have pictures of people with no heads, and a few pictures of nothing but feet. Little ones are not good at aiming a camera, but their photos go in our albums too. One of our grandchildren took a great shot of the Pacific Ocean from the car window while we were traveling. It looks like a windstorm. We share photos of our son Sam and his wife, Karen, on a Harley or our granddaughter Kim in Florida. We even have one of a giant bear in a porch rocker at Myrtle Beach. During the Christmas dinner our family always reminisces about our memorable outings.

All 10 of us have been to Disneyland, Myrtle Beach, Florida, and Christmas musicals. We're planning a trip to Dollywood next year. We suggested Hawaii, but for some reason Elmer doesn't agree.

We're creating memories, a gift to last a lifetime.

—Ruth Towns

Memorable Gifts

One year, I needed a new coffeepot. Elmer, always the tease, bought one for me and wrapped all its pieces separately. The coffee was in a bag tied with a big red bow. Elmer wrapped the stem and basket in a tube from the Christmas paper. The lid appeared in a shirt box. He hid the glass bottom piece in a wastepaper basket. The top glass piece, Elmer placed in a radio box. He got a lot of mileage out of that one gift. But Elmer has a talent for making things a lot more fun than usual. He still hides little gifts in big boxes or wraps light things with a brick. His creativity keeps us guessing.

This Christmas he is not so subtle. Under the tree is a gift that says, "To Ruth, this is for you to puzzle over." When I asked if the puzzle was a bear design, his mouth dropped open in dismay.

—Ruth Towns

He was in the world, and though the world was made through him, the world did not recognize him. He came to that which was his own, but his own did not receive him. Yet to all who received him, to those who believed in his name, he gave the right to become children of God—children born not of natural descent, nor of human decision or a husband's will, but born of God. The Word became flesh and made his dwelling among us. We have seen his glory, the glory of the One and Only, who came from the Father, full of grace and truth.

—John 1:10-14

Christ became like us so that
we could become like Him!

—Mark Toler-Hollingsworth

Personalized Packages

*S*everal years ago I bought white shelf paper to wrap presents. I chose white because our living room is all white, with a white Christmas tree, so white presents seemed appropriate. Then I decided that the gifts needed some color. On Debbie's gifts, I put red bows. On

Polly's, I placed gold bows. And I topped Sam's with blue ribbons and bows. The family easily saw to whom the gifts belonged.

Since then, the colors have changed, but I still wrap all the gifts for the same person the same way. This year, Polly's husband, Ty, gets colored comic-strip paper topped with bright red yarn. Polly gets red paper tied with silver bows. Tammy's packages are wrapped with Winnie-the-Pooh. Our granddaughter, Kim, loves horses. Her packages have beautiful thoroughbreds racing across them. I don't get bored wrapping gifts, and I love to dream up new designs for next time.

And my gifts? Well, Elmer puts mine in gift bags. He says it's much easier than wrapping them.

—Ruth Towns

Christmas is based on an exchange of gifts:
the gift of God to man—
His unspeakable gift of His Son,
and the gift of man to God,
when we present our bodies
as a living sacrifice.

—Vance Havner

The Carrot Slippers

*O*ne year, our daughter Polly bought a pair of slippers to give to our son Sam. They were orange carrots, about three times longer than Sam's feet. We laughed and took pictures of Sam in his carrots. The next year, Ruth unwrapped a beautiful florist's box from Sam, only to be surprised by the same carrot slippers.

Each year, the "keeper of the carrots" decides who will be honored, who will be trusted, to receive this meaningful gift. The slippers are the most desired of all gifts, and we search the packages to see who the lucky person will be. Our granddaughter, Kristen, has them this year, so we are all being so nice to her, wondering whom she will choose. Ruth thinks it's her turn again after 17 years.

—Elmer Towns

As with Gladness Men of Old

As they offered gifts most rare
In that dwelling rude and bare,
So may we with holy joy,

Pure, and free from sin's alloy,
All our costliest treasures bring,
Christ, to Thee, our heav'nly King.

The truth is this—Jesus was a refugee!

In our day, we would call His family indigent or homeless.

—Terry N. Toler

Traveling to West Virginia

Dad had a set philosophy about travel. When we left every Christmas for the long trip to West Virginia, two things were true. The gas tank of the car was full, and our bladders were empty. Dad would travel until those two things reversed, and the gas tank was empty, but our bladders were full.

Sometimes the car would seemingly get miraculous gas mileage, which led to a "complaining spirit" from me and my brothers. At this moment, Mother always encouraged us to sing. A resounding round of Christmas songs distracted us from our discomfort. It was amazing how it worked. We would start to sing and, in short order, forget our weariness and full bladders.

Nevertheless, we were all glad when Daddy finally stopped to gas the car!

—Stan Toler

Light Parades

Thank God, the true Light now shines!
And so long as we walk in its rays,
The darkness cannot overcome it.
This is the message of Advent.

—William M. Greathouse

*S*ometimes I wonder what prompts a person to become the neighborhood spectacle. Every year we look forward to driving by a house on Hill Street, one in Blue Ridge Farms, and the Elk's Home in Bedford, Virginia. At each house, we gaze in amazement and amusement at thousands of gaudy lights illuminating deer and the birdbath; outlining the house and the garage; running up and down the light pole; defining the sidewalk; outlining Santa, his sled, and all eight reindeer; and surrounding the lawn chairs and picnic table. The lights go over and around a Nativity with a snowman nearby. Lights hang in haphazard fashion from bare tree branches, while cardboard carolers with speakers hidden behind them blare out "Winter Wonderland."

We wouldn't miss it for the world. Every year the family piles in one car to view this spectacular display. I wonder whether the residents hide behind the curtains to watch us drive by or if they are in the car behind us.

—Elmer and Ruth Towns

Memory Ornaments

*R*emember the wooden Christmas paint-by-number ornaments? From each child's first Christmas until they were grown, we painted ornaments or purchased dated tree decorations. The 1955 ballerina to the 1975 angel had "Debbie" and the date on them. Polly and Sam also kept track of their ornaments and ritually packed them away until the next Christmas. When each child got married, Christmas-dated ornaments were one of their treasured wedding gifts.

Now Polly's girls love to hang their own keepsake ornaments on the tree. Each year they rediscover the names and dates as did my own children.

—Ruth Towns

A Fabulous Fireplace

*N*ow that our children are raised, gone, and we're on our own, our living room is white. The piano is white. The chairs are white. The armoire in the corner is white. The sofas are white. The brick fireplace is white. The logs are white birch. The mantel and hearth are white. The living-room Christmas tree is white. The wallpaper is white on white.

There's never been a fire in the fireplace. On special occasions, we cover the birch logs with white cloth and haphazardly place white candles in the fireplace. We open the flue and light the candles. It's a fabulous sight! We do it every year.

—Ruth Towns

A Christless Christmas, if such were possible,
would be like counterfeit money.
It might have the appearance, but no real value.

—W. T. Purkiser

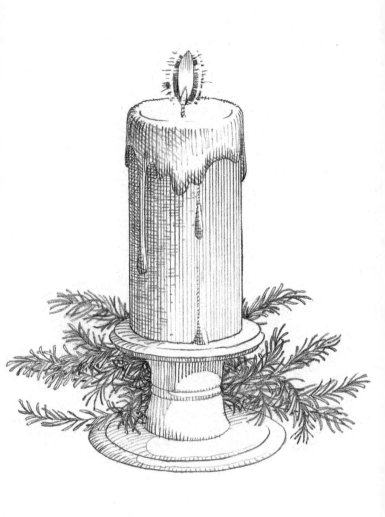

Candles Make Moods

Candles are wonderful mood makers. The big ones last from year to year, but each Christmas I still buy new ones. We group them in threes or fives in every room to give off light and warmth of heart. For larger arrangements, we put the candles at different levels by using boxes or cans as a base. We cover the base with pine, magnolia leaves, and holly. Also, a few ornaments, tucked here and there, catch the candles' reflection. During the Christmas rush, candlelight gently calms children at bedtime or bath time. Furthermore, remember to light fragrance candles an hour before company arrives to delight visitors and set the mood for the holidays.

—Ruth Towns

Counting Christmas Trees

Elmer has a reputation for integrity and character, but his competitive nature puts a chink in his reputation. For example, our family makes a game of counting Christmas trees, and Elmer makes a point of winning. We all pile into the car, and he divides the car into his side and my side. Then we count Christmas trees to determine which side can see the most. A tree doesn't count unless it is decorated with the lights *on*. We drive up and down the streets of Lynchburg, and if a tree is on my side, my team scores. If it's on Elmer's side, his team scores. Should I see the first Christmas tree, Elmer gets competitive.

One night, my team was winning the count. Then Elmer drove around the block to enter the same street from the opposite direction so all the trees would be on the driver's side. We protested loudly. But when Elmer got to the end of the street, he backed all the way down the street so the trees would appear again—all on *his* side.

We still count trees, but now the kids drive!

—Ruth Towns

Christmas is not a myth,
not a tradition, not a dream—
it is a glorious reality.

—Billy Graham

Christmas Clothes

One year we gave Grandpa Forbes a bright red Christmas sweater. He loved it. The sweater seemed to make his snow-white hair even whiter. His cheeks were rosier, and his sparkling blue eyes seemed a more vivid hue. Grandpa Forbes resembled St. Nicholas himself in his special Christmas sweater.

Every December, I unpack my own Christmas clothes—a glittery gold blouse, several decorated sweatshirts, a black sweater with caroling bears on the front, and a gold angel on a long chain. Elmer's green sweater is about as fancy as he gets.

I often wonder if anyone else gets as much pleasure out of Christmas clothes as I do. Just the other day a salesclerk complimented me on the sweatshirt and little silver package earrings I wore. She said it made her day!

—Ruth Towns

Christmas is love in action. Every time we love, every time we give, it's Christmas.

—Dale Evans Rogers

Through the incarnation of Jesus Christ, God opened His arms of forgiveness.

—Elmer Towns

Undecorating

*R*uth was born the day after Christmas. By the time her birthday arrives, we've decked the halls, had several parties, opened our presents, and stuffed ourselves on a sumptuous feast. Family has gathered, and we're all ready to settle down for a long winter's nap.

But what about Ruth? She gets Christmas cards with "P.S. Happy Birthday" on them. She gets leftover pumpkin pie with a candle stuck in it for a "birthday cake."

While the family is together on Christmas Day, it would be convenient for Ruth to open her birthday gifts then. But Ruth cringes at the thought. Her mother began long ago to undecorate on Christmas night, and the tradition continues to this day. By December 26, the tree is down and birthday banners wave. Birthday presents appear, and Christmas wrappings vanish. Bears wear party hats instead of Christmas hats. The house has been undecorated and redecorated.

It's a lot of work, but every year we do the same thing. Oh, did I say "we"? Ruth does it while the rest of us sleep off Christmas dinner.

—Elmer Towns

An Unforgettable Christmas

As for God, his way is perfect;
the word of the LORD is flawless.
He is a shield
for all who take refuge in him.

—Ps. 18:30

Christmas Day, 1961, will always be a memorable day
for the Toler family. Winter had been long and hard
with lots of snow and cold weather. Times were tough!
Dad was laid off from construction work, our food supply dwindled to nothing, and we closed off most of the
house due to our inability to afford high utility bills.

This unforgettable moment really began Christmas
Eve when Mom noted we would have no food Christmas
Day. She suggested that we accept a handout from the
government Commodity Department. So Dad loaded
Terry and me into his old Plymouth and we headed
downtown. That evening we stood in line with others for
what seemed like hours, waiting on the government
handouts—cheese, dried milk, flour, and dried eggs.

UGH!

Finally, Dad could stand it no longer. "We're going home, boys," he said. "God will provide!"

We cried, but completely trusted Dad's faith in God.

That night, we popped popcorn and opened the gifts we had ordered with Mom's Top Value Trading Stamps, saved for Christmas presents. Terry ordered a transistor radio, I ordered a Brownie Kodak camera, and Mark got a baby toy. We were so grateful to have anything!

Everyone slept well under Grandma's handmade quilts that night. Our family was just happy to be together.

On Christmas morning, a loud knock and "Merry Christmas" greetings startled us. The people who attended our church arrived with gifts, clothing, and a 30-day supply of food. Since that day, I have always believed "God will provide." Whenever there is need, He has a prearranged supply to meet that need through His people.

Stan Toler, *God Has Never Failed Me, but He's Sure Scared Me to Death a Few Times* (Tulsa, Okla.: Honor Books, 1995), 18-20.

Pass Traditions to Grandchildren

Jesus, as we close this Christmas season
And look toward the new year,
Help us to become faithful, cross-carrying disciples who
Announce your salvation in and through our daily lives.

—Henri J. M. Nouwen

What do you remember about your grandparents? Were they prim and proper? Did they smell like powder? Did they always have candy in the dish for you?

I really want my children and grandchildren to have great memories of a positive attitude and time to listen to each question or problem. I want them to carry on family values and traditions. I want them to find joy in serving the Lord. I want them to have a marriage like ours. I want them to know they are loved.

I want them to read the books written by their grandfather. I want them to smile when they remember us. I want them to love the Christmas season and remember having fun at our house. I want them to continue the traditions and start some of their own.

—Elmer Towns

Tradition Tips

Tips

* Involve your children in creating "dated" tree ornaments each year.
* Visit shut-ins with the children on Christmas Eve.
* Write your spouse a love letter.
* Teach your children about the symbols of Christmas.

Understanding Christmas Symbols

Around A.D. 200, the first Christian celebrations began in many Christian communities. Over the years, there has been much confusion concerning the use of Christmas trees, ornaments, and decorations of any kind. Stan and I have taught our children the following about the symbols of Christmas:

Tree: Jesus is the Source of everything.

Mistletoe: Jesus is the Prince of Peace.

Holly: Jesus is the Truth.

Lights: Jesus is the Light of the World.

Nativity scene: Jesus is the Reason for the season.

Carols: Jesus is our joy.

Gifts: Jesus is the Giver of life.

—Linda Toler

True Meaning of "The Twelve Days of Christmas"

In 16-century England the meaning of the symbols in "The Twelve Days of Christmas" were as follows:

My True Love: God, the Giver of "every good and perfect gift" (James 1:17-18).

A Partridge in a Pear Tree: Jesus Christ on the Cross (John 10:14-15).

Two Turtle Doves: Mary and Joseph's sacrifice of two doves in the Temple shortly after Jesus' birth (Luke 2:22-24).

Three French Hens: The gold, frankincense, and myrrh given to Jesus by the magi (Matt. 2:10-11, KJV).

Four Calling Birds: Matthew, Mark, Luke, and John, authors of the four Gospels (John 20:30-31).

Five Golden Rings: The Torah, the first five books of the Old Testament (Deut. 34:10-12).

Six Geese a Laying: God, the supreme Creator, made the earth in six days (Gen. 1:1, 31).

Seven Swans a Swimming: The seven gifts of the Spirit—prophesying, serving, teaching, encouraging, giving, leadership, showing mercy (Rom. 12:6-8).

Eight Maids a Milking: The eight Beatitudes (Matt. 5:3-12).

Nine Ladies Dancing: The fruit of the spirit—love, joy, peace, patience, kindness, goodness, faithfulness, gentleness, and self-control (Gal. 5:22-23).

Ten Lords a Leaping: The Ten Commandments (Exod. 20:3-17).

Eleven Pipers Piping: The eleven apostles who were true to Jesus—Simon Peter, James, John, Andrew, Philip, Bartholomew, Matthew, Thomas, James, Thaddaeus, and Simon the Zealot (Mark 3:16-18).

Twelve Drummers Drumming: The Apostles' Creed.

—Debra White Smith

Helen Haidle, *The Real Twelve Days of Christmas* (Sisters, Oreg.: Gold'n Honey Books, 1997).

Tips

✳ Place a basket in the entry for Christmas cards.
✳ Take a trip down memory lane. Look over old Christmas pictures!

* Play Christmas music each evening during the dinner hour.
* Establish a spending budget for each family member.

Budgeting Tips for Christmas

1. Create a budget, and live with it!
2. Plan ahead with a list of things to purchase.
3. Restrict the number of gifts you buy.
4. Plan your shopping time in advance.
5. Take a calculator. Watch the cash register!
6. The day after Christmas, buy gifts for next Christmas at discounted prices.
7. On January 1, start a Christmas account for next Christmas.

Tips

* Hug your family daily.
* Lavishly use room sprays in pine, cinnamon, gingerbread, or vanilla scents.

✳ Repair a broken relationship.

✳ Give thoughtful gifts.

Rings and jewels are not gifts, but apologies for gifts. The only gift is a portion of thyself.

—Ralph Waldo Emerson

Giving Good Gifts at Christmas

GIVE THE GIFT OF LOVE: "How great is the love the Father has lavished on us, that we should be called children of God! And that is what we are! The reason the world does not know us is that it did not know him" (1 John 3:1).

GIVE THE GIFT OF WORSHIP: "Let us not give up meeting together, as some are in the habit of doing, but let us encourage one another—and all the more as you see the Day approaching" (Heb. 10:25).

GIVE THE GIFT OF TIME: "Be very careful, then, how you live—not as unwise but as wise, making the most of every opportunity, because the days are evil.

83

Therefore do not be foolish, but understand what the Lord's will is" (Eph. 5:15-17).

GIVE THE GIFT OF INTEGRITY: "The man of integrity walks securely, but he who takes crooked paths will be found out" (Prov. 10:9).

GIVE THE GIFT OF GOD'S WORD: "These commandments that I give you today are to be upon your hearts. Impress them on your children. Talk about them when you sit at home and when you walk along the road, when you lie down and when you get up. Tie them as symbols on your hands and bind them on your foreheads. Write them on the door frames of your houses and on your gates" (Deut. 6:6-9).

—Stan Toler

Tips

※ Take a drive to a neighboring community to see the lights.

※ Bake cookies for an elderly neighbor.

※ Send cards to missionaries. Be sure to have the whole family sign them. Also arrange to send an offering of love!

※ Give a birthday gift to Jesus in the church Christmas offering.

Wise Worship

*M*y old friend Harry Childers once remarked, "After the wise men had truly worshiped, they opened their treasures." After hearing that, I made an important discovery on my journey to Christmas. You see, I had always wondered what happened to the gifts the wise men brought to the Son of God. Through Harry's observation I was reminded that God's guidance is perfect.

God sent Mary, Joseph, and the Christ child to Bethlehem. When they arrived, they were in great need of food, finances, and shelter. They had moved from the lowly stable to a temporary home. It appeared that Satan's diabolical scheme for Herod to murder babies was going to succeed. But according to my friend Harry, after the wise men worshiped the Savior, they opened their treasures and unwittingly financed the flight of the Son of God to Egypt. Thus, they thwarted Herod's efforts to kill Mary and Joseph's firstborn Son.

Here's my discovery: wise worship always leads to miracles, spiritual breakthroughs, and provisions from the hand of Almighty God! And wise worship only occurs when we, like the wise men, are willing to release our gifts to the Lord. Once that releasing happens, you never know how the Father will use those gifts.

—Stan Toler

Tips

* Place bright red Christmas poinsettias throughout the house.
* Give an anonymous gift to a needy family.
* Write a letter of appreciation to someone who has impacted your life.
* Form a family choir! Sing Christmas carols for your neighbors.

Carols and Cider

Whatever happened to the old custom of Christmas caroling from door to door? It's a welcome sound for us each year when the Oldham family comes around. Then we gather around the piano and enjoy the Christmas carols indoors. Afterward, we sip cider and relish the fellowship of Christian friends.

—Ruth Towns

Deck the Halls

Deck the halls with boughs of holly;
'Tis the season to be jolly.
Don we now our gay apparel;
Troll the ancient yuletide carol.

See the blazing yule before us;
Strike the harp and join the chorus.
Follow me in merry measure,
While I tell of yuletide treasure.

Fast away the old year passes;
Hail the new, ye lads and lasses.
Sing we joyous all together,
Heedless of the wind and weather.

—Welsh Traditional Carol

Tips

✳ Say "I love you" often during the holiday season.

✳ Serve homemade soup and grilled cheese sandwiches.

✳ Give up a bad habit.

✳ Decorate every room in the house.

Deck the Halls . . . and Every Room

*P*ine-scented candles and ribbon-wrapped bathroom tissue are for the green bathroom. Blueberry-scented candles and blue bows are in another bathroom. Cranberry candles serve as part of a centerpiece on the coffee table. Every room in the house is decorated in some way. We use our gold Christmas pillows to add sparkle to the bedroom. The big bow-shaped pillow makes a red, gold, and green "ornament" for a favorite chair.

We like Christmas in every room! We love to deck the halls . . . and the kitchen . . . and the family room . . . and the attic, where the children play! We even hang a wreath on the garage door!

—Ruth Towns

Tips

❊ Help your children create their Christmas wish list.

❊ Take a walk through the neighborhood. Smile at everyone you encounter!

✳ Write a Christmas carol.

✳ Give a Christmas present to your mail carrier.

The Goody Basket

Long ago my mother and father would extend a small Christmas bonus or gift to our regular delivery people. We discovered those special people are often forgotten. We wrap a basketful of small gifts and place them near the front door for the UPS driver, the mailman, the florist, or even neighbors. Usually the mailman will "hand deliver" the mail at the door at least once before Christmas Day. He knows about the gift basket.

We always wrap too many so the children can have a Christmas Eve grab bag with the leftovers. This way, they can "jump the gun" and open gifts before Christmas morning.

—Ruth Towns

Tips

✳ Plan an open house for friends and family.

✳ Volunteer to ring a bell for The Salvation Army.

✳ Dress in bright Christmas colors.

✳ Sign and date your special Christmas treasures.

Faded Place Mats

Not many years ago, if we had Christmas decorations, we made them out of leftovers and imagination. Once, while unpacking Christmas decorations, we found a set of place mats made from woven strips of red and green construction paper. Last year I resurrected napkin rings made from toilet paper tubes and covered with gift wrap and ribbon. I have candleholders made out of tuna cans, covered with mailing cord, and spray-painted gold.

These handmade creations are some of my most treasured possessions. I wish we had signed and dated them. The colors are faded, but once we thought our table the most beautifully decorated one we had ever seen.

—Ruth Towns

Tips

✳ Ask each family member, "If you could only have one gift this Christmas, what would it be?"

* Involve the whole family in decorating the house.
* Give your heart to Jesus.
* Worship together as a family.

Family Advent Worship

The Advent season has become a time of celebration and hope in our home. Each Sunday during Advent, we gather with our sons, Seth and Adam, to worship as a family. We place an Advent wreath on our coffee table. Within the evergreen circle are three purple candles, one rose-colored candle, and a large white candle. The following is our worship schedule:

WEEK ONE: Adam reads Matt. 3:1-2; we light a purple (Prophecy) candle and have family prayer.
Discussion: Expectations and hopes for the future.

WEEK TWO: Seth reads Matt. 2:1-6; we light a purple (Shepherd) candle and have family prayer.
Discussion: Anticipation and preparation for Christmas.

WEEK THREE: Linda reads Luke 2:8-12; we light a rose-colored (Angel) candle and have family prayer.
Discussion: Our joys in life.

WEEK FOUR: Stan reads Matt. 2:7-11; we light a purple (Magi) candle and have family prayer.
Discussion: Good gifts from the Father.

CHRISTMAS DAY: We light the Christ candle and give thanks for Jesus, the Light of the World.

—Linda Toler

Tips

❋ Design a Christmas stocking for each family member.

❋ Call an old friend with a Christmas greeting.

❋ Pop lots of popcorn!

❋ Read the Scriptures daily during the Christmas season (might start a habit!)

The Bible in the Front Hall

Everyone who comes to our home sees the open Bible in the front hall. Sometimes a candelabra or small spotlight illuminates the passage. There's no mistaking that we celebrate the birth of our Savior, our Lord, Jesus Christ.

Somewhere over the years, our son, Sam, acquired a podium-type bookholder. We use it for the open Bible, which is a focal point of the decorations. We highlight the whole account of Jesus' birth so guests will notice it. A beautiful gold cord and tassel serve as a bookmark.

On Christmas Eve, Ruth and I read the Christmas story. Now it's just the two of us, but we still find the account of Christ's birth precious as we read it again and again, year after year, not just as tradition, but because we worship and adore Him.

—Elmer Towns

Tips

✳ Keep an Advent journal.
✳ Write a sentence prayer each day during Advent.
✳ Take lots of pictures at Christmas.
✳ Place candles in the windows of your home.

Williamsburg Candles

Traditionally, Virginians follow the example of Williamsburg and place a single candle in each window. Some colonial homes leave them year round. We began this lovely custom when we moved to Virginia 25 years ago. On December 1, we turn on the electric candles, and they continue to burn day and night for the whole month. Up and down Lynchburg streets the window candles offer a warm, friendly welcome.

Some neighborhoods line the streets with luminaries. This custom came from other countries. The luminaries were thought to light the travelers' way as they came to worship the Christ child.

—Elmer and Ruth Towns

Get a life instead of an eclair.

—Dr. Richard Strait

Dieting Tips at Christmas

1. Read scriptures that focus on perseverance.
2. Sample but don't overeat.
3. Eat three square meals daily.
4. Stick with diet sodas.
5. Discuss your food battles with a fellow struggler.
6. Think about your future with good health.
7. Pray for strength each day.

—Stan "the Always Struggling Dieter" Toler

Favorite Recipes
and
Other Tasty Memoirs

Early Christmas Breakfast

Breakfast at Ty and Polly's home is a special Christmas event. I never want to miss watching our granddaughters, Kim and Beth, open their gifts, so we grab our coffee and head for their house early Christmas morning. Ty says we arrive earlier every year. His parents usually join us within an hour or so, and we start opening gifts.

Stockings come first, then whatever is under the tree. We sip our coffee and watch the kids, then dig into the breakfast goodies. Polly serves a more elaborate breakfast every year. One of our favorite recipes is her quiche.

Polly's Quiche

Spray the bottom of a casserole dish with Pam. Line the bottom with croissants (sliced in half). Cover with a layer of cooked, crumbled sausage (1 lb.) and grated cheese (4 oz.). Pour beaten eggs (6-8) over the sausage and cheese. Salt and pepper to taste. Sprinkle more cheese on top (4 oz.). Bake at 350 degrees for 20 minutes.

Linda's Slushy Punch

2 packages Kool-Aid (any flavor and color you want)
2 quarts water
2 large cans pineapple juice
Sugar to taste
2 bottles ginger ale or 7-Up

Mix all ingredients except 7-Up. Freeze these to a slush.

Just before serving, add the 7-Up.

The first Noel the angels did say
Was to certain poor shepherds
in fields as they lay—
In fields where they lay keeping their sheep
On a cold winter's night that was so deep.

Noel, Noel, Noel, Noel!
Born is the King of Israel!
—Traditional English Carol

Aunt Sue's Peanut Butter Pie

½ cup peanut butter
1 cup powdered sugar
1 baked pastry shell
1 package instant vanilla pudding
1½ cups milk
1 small carton Cool Whip

Combine peanut butter and sugar until mixture is crumbly. Line baked shell with half of mixture. Prepare pudding with milk. Place on top of peanut butter mixture. Top with Cool Whip, and sprinkle remaining peanut butter mixture on top. Chill.

The Christian Christmas Pie

Of all the traditional Christmas foods, mince pie is Christian in origin. The mincemeat represents the frankincense and myrrh the wise men offered at the manger. For centuries the pie was shaped oblong to symbolize the Christ child's manger. So the mince pie calls up images of devout wise men, a humble Bethlehem inn, and the birth of our Savior.

Mince Pie

3 cups cooked pork or beef
3 cups cooked raisins
1 cup cooked apples
1 1/2 cups cooked, dried apricots
1 cup canned peaches
1 cup cherries (canned or frozen)
1 1/2 cups raw apples, chopped
1 cup blueberries or blackberries
1 cup gooseberries (optional)
1/4 cup broth or stock

Cook meat until very tender; cut into very fine pieces. Mix all fruit with meat (peaches and apricots should be cut up in very fine pieces).

For each 9- or 10-inch pie, measure:
2-2 1/2 cups mince
1/2 teaspoon cinnamon
3/4 cup sugar
1 teaspoon apple cider vinegar

If mince is dry, add some peach syrup or fruit juice, then add 2 teaspoons flour to pie mixture. Last, add 1 tablespoon butter.

Bake at 400° for 15 minutes. Lower heat to 375° and bake for additional 45 minutes.

Pappaw Jack's Peanut Butter Fudge

4 cups sugar
1 pound margarine
1 large can evaporated milk
1 cup peanut butter
1 (7 oz.) jar Marshmallow Creme
1 cup nuts

Combine sugar, margarine, and evaporated milk; cook over medium heat until soft ball forms when a drop is placed in cool water. Stir constantly for approximately 30 minutes. Remove from heat; add peanut butter, Marshmallow Creme, and nuts. Beat and pour into buttered 9-by-13-inch pan. Cool and cut into squares.

The hinge of history is on the door
of a Bethlehem stable.

—Ralph W. Sockman

Pa Pa Buddy's Ambrosia

12 or more oranges (juice oranges, or any type)
Coconut to taste (shredded)

Peel oranges. Slice across the section into small pieces. Remove seeds and squeeze remaining juice from the center stem section. Stir in shredded coconut (a little or a lot).

The Cookie Bake Contest

*L*arry and Mary Lou decided to have an annual cookie baking contest that would solve a few problems. Problem No. 1: the kids are always bored, and a contest ends their boredom. Problem No. 2: they want to invite Elmer and me over, but don't have much leisure time during the holidays. Problem No. 3: baking Christmas cookies takes time, and having friends over to help gets the job done quickly.

It's a great evening of fun as adults and kids cram into the kitchen, baking cookies. Many cookie sheets later we stand around the long table still overloaded with bowls, flavoring, chocolate chips, butter wrappers, and candy sprinkles. At this point, we determine who baked the best cookies. The final decision is up to the honorable judge, Elmer Towns, who is honest, impartial, and fair, of course.

Why do Elmer's chocolate-chip cookies always win? He even makes us say in unison, "Elmer's chocolate-chip cookies are the best!"

—Ruth Towns

Mary Christmas

Years ago, our three-year-old wondered if I knew the last name of Jesus' mother. I had to admit that I didn't. He pondered the question a little longer. Suddenly, he brightened and chirped, "I know, Momma. Her name is Mary CHRISTMAS!"

Country Woman Magazine, November/December, 1992.

Ma Ma Carter's Pecan Pie

3 eggs
$^1/_2$ cup granulated sugar
1 cup red corn syrup

3 tablespoons margarine
$\frac{1}{2}$ teaspoon salt
1 teaspoon vanilla
1 cup chopped pecans
1 unbaked piecrust

Beat eggs; add sugar, syrup, margarine, salt, vanilla, and pecans. Mix with a fork. Pour into an unbaked crust, and bake at 375 degrees for 20 minutes; then turn down to 325 degrees for an additional 25 minutes. Nuts will float to the top and form a firm crust. Makes one 9-inch pie. Easy to double or triple.

It came upon the midnight clear,
That glorious song of old,
From angels bending near the earth
To touch their harps of gold.
"Peace on the earth, good-will to men,
From heav'n's all-gracious King."
The world in solemn stillness lay
To hear the angels sing.

—Edmund H. Sears (1849)

Zelda's Rich Chocolate Fudge

4 cups sugar
1 cup butter
1 can (14 oz.) evaporated milk
1 package (12 oz.) semisweet chocolate chips
1 jar (7 oz.) marshmallow cream
1 teaspoon vanilla
1 cup chopped nuts (black walnuts)

In a four-quart microwave bowl, mix sugar, butter, and milk. Cook on high for 20 to 22 minutes or until a few drops of mix in cold water forms a soft ball (234 degrees on candy thermometer). DO NOT LEAVE THERMOMETER IN OVEN WHILE COOKING. Stir well every 5 minutes during cooking. This is a must. Add chocolate chips and marshmallow cream. Stir until well blended. Mix in vanilla and nuts. Pour into buttered 9-inch square dish for thick pieces or 7½-by-12-inch for thinner pieces. Cool and cut.

Question: Why did Mary and Joseph arrive in Bethlehem too late to find a room?

Answer: Because Joseph, like most men, wouldn't ask for directions!

—Adam Toler (15)

A Child's Letter to God

 ear God, did You think that Christmas would turn out like this when You started it? Love, Wendy (age 7).
— *National Reporter,* February 3, 1995

Christmas Eve Dessert First

 ince our kids are all grown and married with families of their own, we have to shuffle the schedules to spend time with each of them. Christmas Eve finds us with our son, Sam, and daughter-in-law, Karen, for dessert buffet. Karen's mom and dad and all the Towns' families enjoy dessert before the big dinner the next day.

This year our granddaughter, one-year-old Collyn, entertained us. Sam and Karen decorated their tree on the top half only so Collyn wouldn't break anything. She couldn't reach the lights and ornaments, but she loved the pumpkin pie and Elmer's favorite pound cake.

Elmer always says his favorite pie is cake. He's different! I guess eating dessert first is a little different, too—but great for making memories!

—Ruth Towns

Linda's Golden Corn Bread

1 ¼ cup self-rising flour
¾ cup self-rising cornmeal mix
2 tablespoons sugar (or less, to taste)
1 teaspoon baking powder
1 egg
⅔ cup milk
⅓ cup salad oil

Measure the flour, meal, sugar, and baking powder in a two-cup measuring cup. Sift into mixing bowl. In same measuring cup, beat egg; add milk and oil. Mix. Pour into flour mixture, stirring with a fork until flour is just moistened. Quickly turn batter into heated, greased iron skillet. Bake 25 to 30 minutes at 425 degrees. Also makes 12 corn muffins. (If using all-purpose flour and meal, increase baking powder to 4½ teaspoons and add 1 teaspoon salt.)

Serving suggestion: great with piping hot homemade vegetable soup!

(P.S. I leave out the sugar when the corn bread is to be used in dressing.)

From the moment of Jesus' conception, undimin-
ished deity and perfect humanity were formed together to make the God-man Jesus Christ.

—Charles F. Stanley

Linda's Corn Bread Dressing

A pan of golden corn bread (recipe on previous page)
1 (14 oz.) bag seasoned shredded-herb stuffing mix
4 or 5 slices day-old wheat or white bread, finely shredded
2 medium to large onions, chopped
1 quart water
Celery (1 bunch, i.e., 6-8 stalks)
Poultry seasoning
Drippings (stock) from the roasted turkey
2 cans (14 oz.) chicken broth

Bake a pan of golden corn bread. When cool,
crumble it finely. Mix stuffing mix, shredded bread
slices, and crumbled corn bread in a large mixing bowl.
Set aside.

Boil chopped onion and celery in a quart of water. When tender, pour water, celery, and onion in a blender and puree. Add pureed mixture to bread mixture and stir.

Add poultry seasoning to taste. Add stock from turkey until mixture is very moist, but not soupy. Use canned broth (referred to above) if needed to get right consistency.

Spray a 9-by-13-inch pan with cooking spray and add dressing. Bake at 350 degrees for 30 minutes (or until slightly brown). Serve smothered with giblet gravy (recipe below).

The Christmas spirit that
goes out with the dried-up
Christmas tree is just as worthless!

—Fred Bock

Linda's Famous Giblet Gravy

Giblet stock
2 tablespoons flour
Canned broth (if needed)

Salt and pepper
Cooked, diced giblets
5 boiled eggs (chopped)

Boil the giblets in 2 quarts of water for 45 minutes to 1 hour. Cool, then debone and chop the giblets.

Pour $\frac{1}{2}$ to 1 cup of giblet stock (and broth, if needed) into a deep skillet. Whisk in flour. Add giblet stock (and broth, if needed) to create desired thickness. Salt and pepper to taste. Bring to a boil. Turn down to simmer. Add diced giblets and chopped eggs. When gravy begins to thicken, remove from heat.

I've got the Christmas blues.
My tree lights blew a fuse.
I don't know which gift to choose.
My charge cards have been refused.
I've got the Christmas blues.

(Sing to the tune of "I'll Have a Blue Christmas")

Ruth's Oyster Stew

Christmas dinner is a combined work of culinary art as each household comes together to bring their favorite addition to the meal. Tammy brings green bean casserole. Debbie bakes the pies. Polly's salads are out of this world, and Karen creates magic with veggies. I cook the turkey and the other specialties. Through the years, we always begin with oyster stew. I'm not really sure if anyone in the family even likes oyster stew, but it's tradition. My mother was from New England and had different ideas about the perfect Christmas dinner. My mother and her mother before her felt that Christmas dinner MUST begin with oyster stew. Since Christmas is tradition, why be different?

—Ruth Towns

The simple shepherds heard the voice of an angel
and found their lamb;
the wise men saw the light of a star
and found their wisdom.

—Bishop Fulton J. Sheen

Seth's Favorite Cinnamon Bread

1 loaf frozen bread (Rhodes or Kroger's)*
$\frac{1}{2}$ stick butter, melted
$\frac{1}{2}$ cup sugar
1 tablespoon cinnamon

Let bread thaw just enough to slice easily (about $\frac{1}{2}$ hour). Cut into 12 pieces. Dip each piece in melted butter and then in sugar-cinnamon mixture. Line in a bread pan and let rise over the top of the pan. Bake at 350 degrees for about 30 minutes. You'll want to make more than one!

*Bread packages give detailed information about regular and quick-rise methods and times.

Adam's Special Apple Drink

Apple juice or apple cider
Cinnamon "Red Hots" candies

For a cup: microwave a cup of juice or cider until hot. Add a teaspoon of cinnamon candies—stir. For a crowd: warm $\frac{1}{2}$ to 1 gallon of juice or cider in Crock-Pot on high. Add about $\frac{1}{2}$ to $\frac{2}{3}$ cup cinnamon candies (more or less to taste). Stir occasionally. Serve hot!

It's a favorite at holidays, or any cold, winter evening, and great with cinnamon bread (previous page).

Doug's Red Wagon

We moved into a neighborhood of three streets all ending in cul-de-sacs. A few days before Christmas, neighborhood men traditionally cooked and delivered goodies throughout the area. I'll never forget the sight of Elmer Towns with packages of cookies and Doug Oldham with jars of soup, packing their treasures in Doug's little red wagon and pulling it door-to-door. When they returned, the wagon was just as full as when they started. The neighbors had loaded the wagon with jars of honey, cranberry bread, jams, and a great hand-decorated ornament.

We loved that neighborhood. People were "real" and a little old-fashioned. They took time to be neighborly, and we knew they were close if we needed them. After we moved, we thought often of them and were thankful we had been included in their love.

—Ruth Towns

Ian Ehrlich (7), son of Rev. and Mrs. Timothy Ehrlich, asked, "Mom, why do people put lights on their houses?"

"They are celebrating Jesus' birthday," she replied.

"When is Jesus' birthday?"

"He was born on Christmas."

"Jesus was born on Christmas? What a coincidence!" Ian exclaimed.

Contributed by Dr. John Bardsley. *Joyful Noiseletter*, December 1994, 2. Used by permission.

Nannie Steedley's Christmas Cake

1 cup sugar
1 cup butter or margarine (2 sticks)
2 cups plain flour (all-purpose)
5 eggs
1 teaspoon lemon
1 teaspoon vanilla
1 quart pecans, chopped
1 pound candied cherries
1 pound candied pineapple
(Or 1 pound white raisins and ½ pound each of cherries and pineapple)

Grease and flour the tube pan.

Mix first 6 ingredients with mixer. Flour the fruits and nuts. Pour batter over fruits and nuts, and mix with hands.

Put a pan of water on the lower rack (this keeps it from browning too quickly). Place cake pan on middle rack. Bake at 250 degrees for 2 hours and 45 minutes or until done.

Storing tip: Wrap tightly and keep frozen.

Serving tip: The frozen cake will slice. It's delicious with a cup of coffee anytime!

Christmastime attains its timelessness.
Eternity is joined with time.

—George W. Cornell

Happy Birthday, Jesus

For a family Christmas dinner, we bake and decorate a large special cake. We display the cake for the children to see. When the children first arrive, we show them the special cake and tell them it is for Jesus' birthday. We also show them a box of birthday candles and tell them, "You can choose a candle and place it on the cake when we sing 'Happy Birthday' to Jesus."

After the meal, we read the story of Jesus' birth. Each child chooses a candle and places it on the cake anywhere he or she desires.

A little guy named Oscar once stuck his candle in sideways, and a wise mother asked why.

"We ought to have lights everywhere for Jesus," he replied.

The candles are lit, all sing "Happy Birthday, Jesus," and together the children blow them out. Like any other birthday party, everyone eats cake.

—Elmer Towns

If you hitch your wagon to a star,
be sure it is the star of Bethlehem!

—Will Rogers

Aunt Mary's Blueberry Salad

1 (20 oz.) can crushed pineapple
1 large package black cherry Jell-O
3 cups hot water
1 can blueberries, drained
1 (8 oz.) carton sour cream
1 (8 oz.) package cream cheese

¹/₂ cup powdered sugar
¹/₂ cup chopped pecans

Drain pineapple and save liquid. Mix Jell-O in hot water, and add pineapple juice. Chill to the consistency of egg whites. Add pineapple and blueberries. Chill until firm. Mix together the sour cream, cream cheese (softened), and sifted powdered sugar. Spread over Jell-O layer. Top with chopped pecans.

The Lord of glory
stooped to be the Babe of the manger
that no proud group of men might ever say,
"He is ours exclusively."

—G. B. Williamson

Mamaw Hollingsworth's Carbonated Salad

Salad
1 (family-size) package lemon Jell-O
2 cups boiling water
2 cups Orange Crush pop
2 to 4 bananas

1 ½ cups miniature marshmallows

1 cup crushed pineapple

Salad instructions: mix Jell-O and water; then add Orange Crush. Add bananas, marshmallows, and pineapple. Pour into 9-by-13-inch pan. Refrigerate overnight.

Topping

1 container (8 oz. or 12 oz.) Cool Whip

2 tablespoons butter

2 eggs

1 cup pineapple juice

½ cup sugar

2 tablespoons flour

Topping instructions: In a saucepan, mix butter, eggs, and pineapple juice. Mix sugar and flour. Add to saucepan mixture. Cook over medium heat until thick. Stir often. Let cool. Add Cool Whip to cooled mixture. Spread over salad.

God's gift to a dying world is a life-giving Savior.
—Talmadge Johnson

Frozen Fruit Salad

My mother and grandmother dreamed up a frozen concoction they made in little metal ice trays. It had fruit cocktail and cream cheese mixed up like ice cream. They sliced it and served it on lettuce leaves. None of us really liked the concoction. But mother served it with so much flourish at dressy dinner parties that we felt like high society eating frozen fruit salad. The little hard, cold pieces of fruit hurt our teeth and once in awhile gave us cold headaches. We smiled and said it was lovely, but we lied. It wasn't good! So when I got married, I continued the charade. Every year, I made frozen fruit salad.

Fortunately, we have somehow managed to lose the recipe. PLEASE DON'T SEND IT TO US IF YOU KNOW IT! We will pass that tradition on to our children in word only. And like all traditions, we'll embellish the good and forget the bad.

—Ruth Towns

Christmas itself may be called into question
If carried so far it creates indigestion.
—Ralph Bergengren

I bought my Christmas cards last January.
I just can't find them.
—Erma Bombeck

Christmas Stories from Elmer and Stan

Stars or Rats?

*J*udy had one small but important part in the children's Christmas party. She was to hold up the word "star" at the appropriate time.

It seemed pretty simple—childproof, if you will. The letters were cut out and attached to a stick. Judy's assignment was to raise the stick with the letters S-T-A-R on it. When the time came, the little girl, right on cue, held the stick high. The audience roared with laughter.

At first the proud mother thought the congregation was appreciating her cute daughter. Then she realized why they were really laughing. You see, no one had told the little girl that there was a right way and a wrong way to hold the stick. Consequently, when she raised the stick, the sign was backward. Instead of saying S-T-A-R, the sign said R-A-T-S.

—Stan Toler

Is Santa Claus Real?

*L*ittle five-year-old Victoria seemed more subdued than normal as her father drove her to school. Her father, Fred, said, "You seem deep in thought. What are you thinking about?"

Victoria replied, "I'm thinking about the Easter bunny."

"Oh really," said Fred, "and what are you thinking about the Easter bunny?"

She said, "Well . . . he's not real!"

Fred thought this might be one of those moments when he could teach the distinction between fantasy and reality. He pressed Victoria with another question. "And what about Santa Claus?"

"Oh, Santa doesn't think the Easter bunny is real either."

—Stan Toler

Christmas Prayers

Christmas had arrived with flourish, and little Jennifer was feeling a lot of pressure. Her father was loaded down with worries and packages. Mom's anxiety had reached the breaking point several times during the day. No matter where Jennifer went, she seemed to be in the way. All around was hustle and bustle, so many trying to do so much, all in an effort to get ready for Christmas.

By the time she was pushed off to bed, the feverish Christmas planning had unnerved her too. As she knelt to pray the Lord's Prayer, she got mixed up and said,

"Forgive us our Christmases, as we forgive those who Christmas against us."

—Elmer Towns

Cash or Credit?

My brother, Terry, often tells about a small girl shopping all day with Grandma. Grandma, seeking good behavior, promised a trip to see Santa at the end of the day. The little girl was good, and the reward was given. Santa gave the little girl a candy cane.

"What do you say to Santa?" Grandma asked.

At first the little girl looked perplexed. Then with a knowing smile she said, "Charge it."

—Stan Toler

Getting Lost in Deep Thought

Robb Robinson, a Tennessee state senator and funeral director, frequently shared humorous stories with me. One such story took place in Nashville.

A local minister, after officiating at a funeral, took

the customary lead car position in the procession to the cemetery. It was during the Christmas season, and the pastor became preoccupied with thoughts of gifts he needed to purchase after the graveside services. When he approached the Spring Hill Cemetery, he looked left and saw the K-Mart store conveniently located across the street. Lost in deep thought, he turned left into the K-Mart parking lot instead of the required right turn into the cemetery. As he drove through the parking lot looking for a parking space, he happened to look in his rearview mirror and saw a string of cars following, all with their lights on!

Stan Toler, *God Has Never Failed Me, but He's Sure Scared Me to Death a Few Times* (Tulsa, Okla.: Honor Books, 1995), 79.

Murphy's Law— Christmas Style

- The time it takes to find a parking place is inversely proportionate to the amount of time you have to spend in the store.

- The more expensive a breakable gift is, the better the chances of dropping it.

- The other checkout line always moves faster.

- Unassembled toys will have twice as many screws as you expect, and some that are supposed to be indispensable will always be left over.

- Interchangeable parts aren't interchangeable.

- All children have built-in detection devices when it comes to finding the Christmas gifts you've so cleverly hidden.

- Amnesia strikes all family members when trying to find the Scotch tape and scissors.

- When a broken toy is demonstrated for the store manager, it works perfectly.

—Anonymous (via E-mail)

Christmas Stage Fright

Little four-year-old Johnny was scheduled to make his first appearance on stage at the Christmas program. He was to quote John 3:16. After much practice he was ready to step on the platform and quote his verse. As the spotlight zoomed in on Johnny, he froze for a moment, smiled broadly, and said, "For God so loved the world, that he gave his only forgotten Son . . ."

—Elmer Towns

Who's Having What?

My brother, Pastor Mark, enjoys telling a Christmas story about a father picking up his son after Sunday School at Edmond First Nazarene Church.

"What did you learn today in Sunday School?" asked the father.

Being used to such inquiries, four-year-old Junior was ready to respond. He had made an angel finger puppet to announce Jesus' birth. He placed the puppet on his finger and proudly proclaimed, "Good news! Good news! Jesus is having a baby!"

—Stan Toler

Room at the Inn

George Goldtrap loves to tell the story about a first grade class presenting its Nativity play shortly before Christmas. As the story goes, Joseph knocks on the door of the inn asking if there are any rooms available. The little innkeeper quickly responded, "You're lucky. We just had a cancellation."

—Elmer Towns

The Wise Men's Gifts

One Christmas Mrs. Johnson was dramatically retelling the story of the three wise men who brought gifts to Jesus. She paused and asked the class, "What gifts did they bring?"

One bright third grader said, "Gold, frankincense, and myrrh!"

To which little Susie, who had just acquired a new baby brother, said, "That's great, but what Mary really needed was diapers!"

—Stan Toler

Conclusion

What Makes Christmas Perfect?

As a little girl, I thought Christmas was perfect the year I received my shiny green and silver Western Flyer bicycle. I had slipped out of bed on Christmas Eve night to sneak a peek at gifts under the tree. However, I was halted at the door by an eerie, yet wonderful, gleam from the living room. Something was reflecting the moonlight from the window. The next morning, I discovered my beautiful bike. I probably rode it thousands (well, maybe hundreds) of miles over the ensuing years. Only after I was married did I finally part with it. The bike had once been so perfect, but it became rusty and useless.

As a young teen, I thought the perfect Christmas was spent at my grandparents' home on Christmas Day. All the cousins were there, and we could find many amusements on that old south Georgia farm. Nanny always made roast turkey with two kinds of dressing, two other meats, and a multitude of fancy delicacies. There was always a huge pot of mustard greens. (I love them!) But now both of my grandparents are gone. The old farmhouse has been sold. The Christmases at that country home seemed perfect, but now they are only treasured memories.

As a young adult, I remember the adventure of my

first Christmas with my husband, Stan, and his family. We were engaged to be married. Life was wonderful. We were in love. The perfect Christmas! But, even so, I spent that Christmas away from my parents for the first time. I remember Mother cried when I gave her a very crude, little clay pitcher I had made in a college art class. I realize now that couldn't have been the perfect Christmas, if separation and sadness marred it.

Now, I think I have a better understanding of what makes the perfect Christmas. Age, occupation, or social position don't matter. All that really counts is the relationship I have with Jesus Christ.

For the perfect Christmas, we must experience Jesus as our Lord and Savior.

—Linda Toler

The Light of the World Is Jesus!

L The people walking in darkness have seen a great LIGHT; on those living in the land of the shadow of death a LIGHT has dawned *(Isa. 9:2)*.

I But IF we walk in the light, as he is in the light, we have fellowship with one another, and the blood of Jesus, his Son, purifies us from all sin *(1 John 1:7)*.

G The people living in darkness have seen a GREAT light *(Matt. 4:16)*.

H In HIM was life, and that life was the light of men *(John 1:4)*.

T THE TRUE light that gives light to every man was coming into the world *(John 1:9)*.